BY DEREK O'NEILL

Stress

ISBN: 978-1-936470-39-6
First Edition

Get a Grip Series © 2015
Editor: Nancy Moss
Front Cover Design: © 2015 by Derek O'Neill

DEDICATION

To all who read this book, I salute you for wanting to change the way you live for the better and for having the courage to be who you are as fully as possible.

To all who encourage me everyday to keep going and sharing their lives with me, family small and large. But most of all the little angels who came to teach me – Alexa and Blake, my grandchildren.

"Everybody hurts sometimes, and when we do it is nice to have Derek O'Neill around. His excellent little books on the things that get us, (fear, anger, depression, victimhood, mental blocks) allow us to find our way safely through our psychological minefields and arrive safely at the other side. Read them when you need them."

Paul Perry, Author of the
New York Times Bestseller
Evidence of the Afterlife

TABLE OF CONTENTS

AUTHOR'S PREFACE

Thank you for purchasing *Stress – Is Stress Stressing You Out?* This book has not come about as a result of my training as a therapist, but through some hard-earned lessons that I have experienced myself. This is how I know the path out of limiting beliefs and behaviors that hinder growth. The tools that I offer in this book have worked not only for me, but also for hundreds if not thousands of other people. I have shared these ideas and techniques in my workshops, one-on-one sessions, video and radio broadcasts, and on my website, and I have witnessed astounding results time and time again. Through observation of others, and myself, I have learned to identify the triggers and root causes of disharmony. Most of all, I have come to understand and apply the best methods for achieving peace and balance in life; not perfection, but real transformation and harmony that comes with learning who we are and what makes us tick. My 35 years of martial arts study has given me a refined sense of timing for when to strike with the sword to cut away old patterns, and when to use the brush to paint the picture of the life we deserve and can have.

The 'Get a Grip' series of books offers tangible, authentic wisdom that can help you in all aspects of your life. You've made a great choice by investing in this book. Enjoy the read, and take time to learn and apply the techniques. Let's change who we are together.

Derek

Stress

Is stress stressing you out?

IS STRESS STRESSING YOU OUT?

Have you ever come back from a "relaxing" vacation more tense and anxious than when you left? Do you talk about how stressed you are, but feel too overwhelmed to do anything about it? Is worry and exhaustion your constant companion? Is the stress in your life stressing you out?

There's no denying that life presents its challenges, but the pressure we put on ourselves, and the constant "noise" of our society, causes even more stress. The effects of stress can be obvious, or they can build slowly under the surface. It takes a conscious effort to turn down the volume, look at the bigger picture, and think about what is truly important to us.

The stress management industry is worth billions of dollars because most people don't understand how to truly "switch off," renew, and recharge. There is even more money being spent by companies to keep you in a never-ending stream of distractions and diversions. We hear the message that if we switch off we'll miss something, fall behind, or lose. Often we don't even know what the race is truly about, yet feel it's important that we "win" it.

We live with many expectations and responsibilities, along with technology and other forms of stimuli that keep us wired – sometimes literally! Many people are afraid to get off the cycle of a stress-inducing mindset, and yet its fallout can keep us from what we really need to be happy. Ironically, learning to do less can actually bring more to your life. We work and play better when we prioritize, simplify, and focus.

Negative feelings thrive in the atmosphere of tension and anxiety, and the long-term effects can be very detrimental to your overall health. "Switching off" means to stop, look at what is truly important, and tap into self-care and compassion. You must make a conscious decision to deal with stress as it arises. You need to plan your life in a way that allows you to move through the inevitable challenges we all face – big and small – with calmness and serenity.

Before you can do anything about the stress you are feeling, you have to commit to inviting peace into your life. You do that by giving yourself the space to breathe, setting your priorities, and shifting your attitude about how you want to experience every event and situation that you encounter. You must give yourself the gift of time to do that. No matter how busy you may be, or how many responsibilities you are juggling, you have to take care of yourself first. This isn't greedy or selfish. You cannot help anyone until you help yourself. Stress competes for your time and your heart. The better you handle it for yourself, the more you have to give.

In the pages that follow, I will talk about creating a peaceful lifestyle, shifting your perspective, finding time for yourself, the mind-body connection of stress, and many other topics. So sit back, relax (at least while you read!), and begin the journey to less stress and more tranquility...

CREATING A LIFESTYLE OF PEACE – THE ECOLOGY CHECK

Our minds are very powerful. We may not be able to remove the frustration and tensions in some of our interactions with people, places, and things, but we can shift our approach and our reactions. When you try to control a situation or person outside of yourself, stress is sure to follow. With various teachings and techniques, real change is possible.

The best way to start to heal from constant stress is to realize that we have nothing to prove to anyone else. We must learn to deal with other people in our lives - family members, friends, and strangers - yet you can't take on other people's problems or expectations. Conflicts, complications, and various unwelcome events and feelings will always show up. If you take responsibility for yourself, and stop living for external approval or attention, you'll be closer to transforming and letting go of your stress. Do you invite stress in because of your mindset? Do you fear judgment from others? Do you shape your choices by things and ideas that aren't truly your own? These are recipes for stress.

We can create a lifestyle of peace, no matter what our circumstances look like. No one else is able to do that for you. If you place yourself in a position of victimhood, you are going to be out of harmony with the world. Most of our triggers are formed in experiences from childhood. We can choose to react to them in either a peaceful way or a non-peaceful way. When an event happens in your present-day life you have control over how you respond. It can be as simple as being stuck in traffic and accepting that stressing about it doesn't get you where you're going any sooner, to bigger issues like stress over your finances, especially if connected to feelings from past family dynamics. Realistically, is the stress going to help change your situation? We know it won't, but we fall back into stress so easily, fueled by fear.

We have a conscious and a sub-conscious mind. Though we are consciously aware of what we're doing - or think we are - it's our unconscious mind that's running most of our being. If you feel you are unworthy of a peaceful lifestyle, that belief needs to be looked at and changed. We have the ability to activate both the positive and negative messaging in our brain. Our negative thoughts won't disappear entirely, but greeting them with acceptance, and then activating positive messaging will help to ward off stress. One of the most positive mindsets you can have is accepting that you cannot control the external world, only yourself.

When we do an "ecology check," we look at our beliefs and how they affect us. What have you come to believe as the truth? Do you think all will be perfect if you lose 20 pounds and when you only lose 10, do you become angry at yourself (and maybe put back all the pounds and more?) Is repeatedly thinking about the possible negative outcome something you believe you have to do in order to prepare for "the worst?" Is staying in constant touch with everyone, online or on the phone, the only way you feel connected? Where do these beliefs come from? What happened in the past, or more recently, that set this "ecology" as something that feels natural to you, even when it's an illusion?

Beliefs create your world – and shape how much stress you will encounter. We see how the beliefs people hold can cause conflict in families or workplaces, and even on a large scale when it comes to wars and global strife. It all starts with the self. Every one of us is made up of energy, and that energy cannot be destroyed. We are attracted to pleasure and averted by pain. When an event happens we're going to react one of two ways, positively or negatively. If you're involved in a fender-bender, you can jump out of the car and ask the people in the other car if everyone is safe and unharmed. That positive approach will probably get a positive, less stressful response. If you jump out of your car screaming and shouting, chances are you'll be met with the same. It's up to you to decide what way to respond to anything that happens. You've hit the car and can't undo that!

Think about the ecology of your thinking. Is it geared toward peace or conflict? For example, have you come to believe that there is only one way to deal with a family member you have a troublesome relationship with, perhaps by enduring their criticism or unhealthy dependence on you? How can you change these stressful dynamics through your reaction to them? You will drive yourself into a dark tunnel of stress trying to change the person. The key lies with you.

On a smaller scale, do you believe that traveling on a plane is always stressful, no matter what? What can you do to alleviate the stress you feel you can't avoid? It can be as simple as preparing and choosing differently. Maybe you need to make sure you book an aisle seat, bring water onboard, and wear a sweater to take on and off to combat the annoying temperature changes. We can preempt what we need in our ecology in order for peace and harmony to seep in. A lovely plant on your desk at work, a kind word to someone who troubles you, or a deep breath when you feel overwhelmed. There is always something you can do to create a peaceful mindset.

Checking your ecology also means paying attention when something is wrong. We tend to brush things under the rug and stick our heads in the sand. The buried feelings bubble up as stress. Become open to the idea that the universe is giving you very clear messages that something is right or wrong. You don't have to always act on your gut feeling, but you must acknowledge that feeling.

Try to sit quietly for 5 or 10 minutes every day and think about what is stressing you and why. If you process the information that is revealed, you will begin to feel much more confident and powerful about yourself. You'll be able to stand up and say, "sorry, this is not for me" or "that works for me." Your decisions will be clearer and stronger, based on your own experience and not somebody else's. The stress will begin to subside and take a backseat in your life.

OUR ADDICTION TO TECHNOLOGY AND THE PRESSURE COOKER OF LIFE

We live in a world where communication and the availability of information has reached a level that people never could have imagined just a generation ago. For all the benefits of technology, the effect of its ever-present force has changed our society in ways that contribute to stress. We feel we have to be available all the time, respond immediately, and be on top of everything that's going on. The expectations are ratcheted up and the old ways of communication, person-to-person, are fading.

Social media, though wonderful in its ability to bring us together, can distract us from real life and interaction, make us feel inadequate, and steal from our downtime when we should be recharging. You may not even realize how dependent you are on that smart phone and the internet, or that it affects your level of stress. Between the constant stimulus and the isolating aspect of everyone staring into their smart phones, we are losing human connection and awareness of our surroundings. When you are overstimulated and cut off from others, it is likely that you'll feel stressed.

Much of our culture is geared toward making you feel "less than." Articles and ads tell you that you're too fat, too skinny, how you're not parenting properly, why tomatoes give you cancer, and how if you don't eat enough tomatoes, you'll get cancer! The internet has made all this noise much louder. No one is going to shut down that clamor for you; it's all around us. You have to take action to make changes.

Ask yourself – how often do I really have to check my email? Am I turning to the internet for information that I really need? How much time am I spending on these devices? What can I replace with something that I can truly benefit from? How, overall, has my daily routine changed because of technology? How realistic, or necessary, is the messaging and information I'm getting from the constant barrage of advertising and technology? Though I'm sure there are many truly helpful and positive effects for you, look at the harm that too much technology can cause.

Along with technology, the many choices, decisions, and responsibilities we take on can be overwhelming. If you want to relieve pressure from your life, come out of the pressure cooker. What is it that's causing you to feel pressurized by society? What can you change in your own life? You don't have to drop everything or make a huge shift in your circumstances, but you do need to see what you can leave behind, and how to look at what is truly important to you with a new perspective. In order to alleviate stress, you must prioritize. It's impossible to do everything, especially if you are spending all your time doing things for other people.

We fear letting go of what we know and have become accustomed to, even if it is hurting us. Too often, the stressed out person is someone who feels they need to be challenged and tested all the time. They may think they will be rejected by a person or fired from a job if they don't reach a level of perfection. The stress only makes that feeling grow. You can change this pattern by asking yourself questions about the source of your stress, and separating the messaging that your mind is giving you from reality.

Anger, resentment, and past hurt can play a role in stress. When we fail to understand our anger and let go, it lives on subconsciously. Situations arise that trigger anger and cause us to overreact. Maybe something your boss said to you reminds you of a parent's criticism. Perhaps your current partner inadvertently acted in a way that sparked the memory of a painful event from a past relationship. The way you react to these triggers with stressful emotions could very well manifest in a very negative way. All perception is projection. The way we see our world has to do with how our perception has been formed. You may have even learned from a continually stressed parent that anxiety is an unavoidable part of life.

When your world feels like a pressure cooker, it is important to always come back to positive thoughts. No matter how stressful and chaotic things may seem, know that life is perfect in the way it unfolds in the bigger picture. We don't have to know everything in order to keep a positive outlook. Sometimes you need to search deep for the unseen benefit of the dark cloud. Once you find contentment in a spiritual practice that connects you to a higher truth, nothing of any value can be taken from you – it resides inside.

All you have to do to be happy is to let go of worry and negativity. That may sound simplistic but it's true. The hard part is turning those feelings over. Happiness and a stress-free life isn't a perfect one. There will always be days where you're feeling more down than up. Events will happen that rattle your faith in everything that is good. It always comes back to what we can control and what we can't. The hardships, disappointments, and heartaches are unavoidable, but long-term, destructive stress can be.

Our mind is creating our reality, and stress is our choice to have or not. Negative thoughts must be corrected all the time, otherwise they grow. If you beat yourself up for making mistakes, you're going to make more mistakes. Whatever your mind focuses on that's what you create. If you focus on negativity, you'll get more of it. That's why you see people go into spirals. They lose their job and then they lose their confidence, instead of saying to themselves, "that's great; there must be a better one around the corner." You have to put energy into shifting your responses. Stress is counterproductive, draining you of the very thing you need to combat it!

TIME TO YOURSELF

We are all different in terms of what we need to decompress from stress. Though the common bond is that we have to change our thinking about the tensions and triggers in our lives, the practical lifestyle tools can vary. One person may find a walk in nature the best remedy. Another person lets off steam by talking to a friend and sharing what they're feeling. It takes observation and self-knowledge to find out what truly works for you. After a stressful day, you might need to go into a room for five minutes of quiet before you speak to your family. Communicating your needs is a large part of dealing with stress. Misunderstanding can lead to more tension.

If you don't take time for you, in whatever way works best, the stress will snowball. So many people are not in touch with what helps them to feel more relaxed and calm. They use the excuse that they're too busy and it's not worth the effort to find out. Some feel undeserving of taking time out, or activities that relax them. If this sounds familiar, you need to examine where that emotion comes from. If you don't ask for what you need, you certainly won't get it. Taking on more work than is humanly possible, trying to be in more than one place at a time, or spending money you don't have on someone is going to have a detrimental effect down the line.

Alleviating stress is dependent on learning to say "no." We get caught up in the feeling that we can't say no to people in our lives, thinking they will be disappointed, or angry, or perhaps even stop loving us. We operate from a place of fear. If you allow people around you to deplete your energy, eventually you'll have none left for you, or for them. No matter how important they are to you, you aren't doing anyone any favors when you extend yourself beyond your capabilities. Taking good care of others can only happen when you've taken care of yourself. When you communicate your needs, you will receive cooperation. The people in your life will feel that they're playing their part in helping you, just like you help them.

You cannot always oblige, but you can always speak obligingly. Here's an example of what that means. When someone asks me to give them a lift to the airport at four in the morning, if I say yes I'll be tired and off-kilter for two days. When I go to the airport, which is very regularly, I never ask anybody to give me a ride that early. I will always get a taxi. So, what did I say to the person who asked me to take them at 4 a.m.? I said my truth – that I'd feel the effect for days - and that if they had a problem with it, I'd pay for their taxi. The idea that you can't always oblige, but you can always speak obligingly is so very important. If you don't have the ability to say that to somebody, you have issues around needing to be needed. Instead of being confident about who you are, independent of anyone else, you're basing your importance on another person's dependency on you. Needing others is a wonderful manifestation of our human connection, but not when it crosses over into territory that diminishes your truth.

Time for yourself is not just the minutes (or hours if you are lucky!) you carve out in order to regroup and recharge, it's the time you take to stop and ask yourself what you need to function at your best without stress, and thrive.

QUIETING THE CRITICAL VOICE AND THE MIND-BODY CONNECTION OF STRESS

One of the major sources of feeling stressed out is self-criticism. Two people could experience the same set of challenging responsibilities in their lives, yet have very different mindsets affecting how much stress they will feel. One will beat themselves up with the critical voice in their head – adding to the stress - and the other will speak with kindness and compassion towards the stress and let it go. How we talk to ourselves has a huge effect in how we handle small daily frustrations, along with the bigger challenges we face. Think about the harsh ways you may be talking to your stress, versus the nurturing, self-loving voice. Your inner voice is more powerful than the outer voice.

We also need to think of our timeline. Are you looking back or off to the side, confused and distracted, or do you see your life as going in a forward direction? A timeline that is forward facing creates more positivity and stops the critical mind. You have to know that your future is the line in front of you. If you don't send your mind in the right direction it will misguide your energy. That's why people get sick from stress. Moving your timeline forward keeps you focused on the bigger picture and the reality that life is always changing. Living in a way that propels you to the next circumstance or emotion – whatever that may be – will center your energy.

Though everyone is looking to feel less stress in their lives, you could actually be embracing it. If you keep saying, "I'm so stressed out," your conscious mind will try to prove it so. When we are convinced of something, we seek it out and find it. Instead of almost literally spinning out on stress, if we stop, take a deep breath, and sit quietly, we can begin to look at the truth behind our projections on to other people, events, or things. The next time you convince yourself that there is no remedy to the stresses in your life ask yourself, "Is there truth in that, or is it just my ego looking to gratify itself?"

There is a strong mind-body connection within us. Stress is a perfect example of how the body is affected by the mindset you embody. Stressful situations trigger the neurotransmitters that send messages from one cell to the next cell. Our body holds memory in our cellular system. Along with the fact that you are probably not going to take care of yourself in the best way possible when you are stressed, there is a lot going on at the cellular level, which can show up as serious health conditions. Cells seem to send memories to each other, which is why people who are getting things like massage, reflexology, touch therapy, and acupuncture, may begin to feel a flood of emotion and even cry. A memory is locked into a cell, and when it's being touched, it releases.

Your neurons and cells – and your body as a whole – are listening in on your self-speak. They send that message onto the next cell, which takes it onto the next cell and so on, multiplying either the positive message you give yourself, or the negative one. As soon as you've enveloped yourself in some sort of negativity, it's important that you counter it with positive self-speak. You body listens to your mind and you have the choice as to what kind of conversation you want to have with it.

ANCHORING, OBSERVATION, AND LOOKING AT THE BIG PICTURE

If we take more responsibility for what is going on in our lives – including how we handle stress - we can change it for the better. We have all learned to blame somebody or something for our problems, whether it be a person or event from the past, or our present-day circumstances. You can't change the past, and there are situations that aren't going away tomorrow, but you can affect your future by how you see your role in the bigger picture of your own life. Stress keeps that picture very small, not allowing you the perspective you need.

Focus and concentration are important abilities that help us do what we want or need to, and yet, if we lose sight of what truly matters, and stress about things that are inconsequential in the end, we'll never find harmony. Is it necessary to finish that entire task today? Will your friend hold a grudge if you say you can't help her right now? Will the delay at the airport go any faster if you get angry, frustrated, or stressed out? In the big picture, isn't your peace of mind, and your health, more important?

We learn by observation. Staying present in each moment is key, but with the ability to look at the context of why we may be reacting a certain way, or feeling a particular emotion. When you're in the thick of stressful emotions, it's very difficult to make a clear decision. When you're angry and anxious, that's not the time to have an important conversation with somebody. That's a battle, not a conversation! The ability to step back and observe what is happening to you at any given moment is empowering. The next time you feel stressed, try stepping back. It will take practice, but in time the reflex of observation can become automatic.

The reason why people routinely pray, meditate, or have a contemplative discipline is to learn a way to always find a calm space. When something triggers them and they need to know the way back to serenity, they can tap into it at any time. You have to train your mind and body to know when stress is becoming overwhelming. I like to use the exercise of bringing my two fingers together – fingertip to fingertip. As soon as they touch, a memory that I have put into my psyche of being happy, joyful, and positive is released to combat my stress. This is called anchoring. The next time you feel very happy – such as that sunny day at the beach eating ice cream - quiet yourself for a minute, and then do something physical such as touching your fingers together. When you feel stressed, you can anchor back to the happy memory by repeating the physical action you have chosen.

We can create our own future by looking at the foundation that our beliefs are built on. How you handle life's stresses is a reflection of your programming. If you believe that you are a victim, you will continue to suffer. We're not targets of anyone or anything. We only become victims when we allow somebody to do that to us. You must begin to look at everything in a holistic way, rather than fixating on things you cannot change. You are in charge of your own feelings. The demands of a relative or friend, or a jam-packed schedule of tasks, or the high demands of a job, are outside of you. Your reactions are within your power to shape.

When you step back from your stress and the emotions that come with it, you are practicing positive detachment. If there are changes we can make, such as learning to say "no," or not over-scheduling ourselves, or looking for help with a task that has us extended beyond our ability, we can lower our stress. Yet no matter how much or how little the shape of our external life can be rearranged, the internal shift is the most important. The same events and situations that cause you stress can be emotionally detached from in a healthy way. Detaching doesn't mean you no longer care, or that you are just going through the motions. It means that you don't allow the external world to trigger you. When stepping back from negative emotions becomes a new habit, you begin to clearly see that you have a choice in how stress affects you.

One of the greatest things that we can do for ourselves at this time is begin to consciously detach from expectations. We think that we have certain material things, or are in a perfect relationship, or high-powered job. All of this causes suffering and stress. Nothing or no one else makes you whole. To be whole you have to find harmony within yourself. Stop and ask, "Who am I? What am I doing here? What are we born for? Is there something more to all of this?"

Your strength – and ability to deal with stress - comes from remaining open to all the experiences that life has for you. When you get to a stage where you begin to stop tagging those experiences as good or bad, and you just call them experiences, that's when stress disappears and happiness flows.

Recognize your feelings and vulnerability, acknowledge the stress, and know that it is all part of life. Vulnerability is one of the greatest strengths a person has. If you are vulnerable, you will never be hurt. It is the opposite of fear. Think about the roots of your stress beyond the actual situation or person that seems to be the cause of it. Are you operating from a place of fear, or are you embracing your vulnerability and fragility? When you embrace it instead of fighting it, you can let go of stress. Vulnerability is having the courage to say to people, "I am not perfect."

TIPS AND TOOLS TO DE-STRESS

Using many of the ideas I've outlined in the previous pages, the following are strategies I've used and recommended to others for alleviating stress, with excellent results. Stress is one of the major issues in our daily lives. It affects us on a personal scale, and collectively. The world we live in would improve if more people would practice these concepts.

- Pack lightly – The symbolism of packing lightly for a trip is one that works well for the bigger picture of your life. The less "stuff" you have, the more likely it is that you'll be happy in a lasting, true way. When you possess many things, you need to keep acquiring more. There never seems to be enough. The stress of feeling that way, and chasing after it, takes it toll. It is based on illusion. We need to get in touch with what makes us happy – our mindset, not our things. What good are the big house and fancy car if you are going to run yourself into the ground going after them? Think about what you need vs. what you think you want. Do you assume your kids would rather have the expensive toys you have to work around the clock to afford, or quality time with you?

- Packing lighter is also an attitude shift. When you simplify your external world, you also clean out space in your psyche. What expectations and pressures can you let go of that will not only free your time and attention, but ease your overall way of thinking? Is there clutter in your mind? Are there problems you feel you must solve today or plans you have to nail down immediately? What are the consequences if you don't? Probably nowhere near as dire as you think while in a state of stress. Make decisions from a calm place. Clean out your physical world and your mindset.

- Know your limits – There is only so much time each day. We all have certain strengths and abilities, but also limitations. It is okay that your house isn't sparkling clean, or that you couldn't volunteer for that committee, or that you had to leave work early to take care of your child. Do you know how to say "no" to situations and people when you need to? Learn to communicate "no" in a way that is kind and understanding, but clear. When you feel stressed out, tell yourself that you are doing the best you can. Stressing over things that are beyond your limits is destructive.

- Limits are not weaknesses; they are boundaries that you need, and it's your responsibility to figure out what they are for you. Knowing how much you can help someone else gives you a clear understanding of when you have to "switch off" and concentrate on self-care. If you allow people to continue to ask you for more and more - and you keep giving it to them - you're going to achieve nothing except excellent stress!

- Review and acknowledge - Here's something I do every night and recommend: When you go to bed take five minutes and review your day. Ask yourself was there anything you could have done better, or differently. Could you have said something more kindly? Just acknowledge it and let it go. Chances are you'll go to sleep faster and be able to rest better. Stress can build by the end of the day. If you don't relieve yourself of it, your sleep will be disturbed and you'll be tired the next day – and more susceptible to stress. Ask your mind to deal with anything that's upsetting or negative going on in your life. Give your mind permission to process these things while it sends your body to sleep, and then ask if it would be kind enough to wake you up in the morning!

- Check your responsibilities - Look at anything you feel responsible for and make sure that you actually are. Not all the tasks that you are doing now are necessarily your burden. There are probably things that you could ask for help with, but you must learn to give up control and delegate. Reaching out for help can save your energy for important responsibilities that you need and want to fulfill. Do you devote a lot of mental energy worrying about other people? Are these your burdens, or the other person's responsibility? There comes a time when you must separate the two. It's hard when a family member or close friend is having a hard time and we want to help. Be mindful that when helping them starts hurting you, you must step back.

- Simplify and clean out your technology – Something else I do regularly is look at my phone numbers. Going down the list, if I haven't called a particular number in a year – or they have not called me – I take it off my contacts. Though a small step, the idea that you don't need to be in touch with everyone from every part of your life is a strong symbol of "switching off" and focusing in on what is important. The same is true for your social media. Are you collecting friends there, rather than working on your true friendships, and forming new, substantial bonds? Our social media profiles are wonderful ways to connect and rediscover; yet they can also be a source of competition and bad feelings. Decide what you can let go of. Is participating in social media causing you stress? Take a break and you'll probably find that you really don't need it as much as you thought you did. Turn off your phone, turn off the news, and turn off the noise. Find time in your day to look inward rather then spending untold hours viewing the world through technology. At the very least, shut down your technology at the end of the day, about an hour or two before you go to sleep. No one should be calling you after 10 p.m. There's usually no pressing matter that needs to be taken care of at that time. Ease into a restful state of "switching off" at night.

- Diet and exercise have a strong affect on stress. Eat healthy foods in moderation. Don't worry about a maintaining a perfect diet, but know that good food will regulate digestion and support your immune system, both easily thrown off by stress. Although finding time to exercise may seem impossible, physical activity is so important. The endorphins released by exercise are a natural antidote to stress, and feeling physically healthy supports your mental strength. Alcohol and drugs may seem like stress relievers, but they easily worsen your anxiety over time. Watch your caffeine intake. Drinking too much coffee over the course of the day can sneak up on you and magnify the feelings of stress. Overall, self-care is one of the most important areas to look at if you are attempting to reduce the stress in your life.

- Laugh more – Though stress can have serious consequences, laughing – even while going through a challenging time - gives you the opportunity to step back and lighten your mood. Through laughter, you can gain perspective and create the kind of energy that tackles stressful times in your life. Laughter is always a wonderful therapy!

MEDITATION AND AN EXERCISE FOR STRESS RELIEF

There are wonderful practices available to you that combat stress. Yoga, massage, martial arts, and a multitude of other activities and disciplines can help you tremendously. Meditation is especially helpful for calming the mind and allowing it to go deeper, beyond whatever is stressing you out. Sitting still in a quiet space and breathing deeply, even for a few moments, will create a feeling of safety and security while improving your health and well-being. Light a candle and watch it for five minutes. Your stress will disappear and bliss will become a natural part of your life.

We should always try to give ourselves something that costs nothing, and meditation is a perfect gift. When you want to get to the bottom of issues and problems in your life, go into a meditative state by sitting quietly and closing your eyes. Reach the point where you are relaxed and have flushed your mind of all the "noise." That's the time to ask the questions about the source of your stress, for example, "Why is it that I always fail when taking a test, even though I know the answers?" "Why is it that every time I lose weight I put it back on, and twice as much?" Your mind will begin to show you and tell you that the reason you are putting on weight is because you are trying to protect yourself, or that your shoulders are tight all the time as a way of protecting your heart. You'll be amazed at how much wisdom is built within your own system. Your mind can give you the answers to very deep-seated issues in your life. Meditation is a ticket for that journey. Take time to practice it at a time and place that suits you best.

Here's an exercise to alleviate stress and help you remove an external problem or situation from your internal thoughts:

Pick an issue that you might currently be having – a fight with a friend, a financial challenge, a health problem, etc. Take a deep breath and as you exhale, close your eyes. If you're a visual type, "see" that person, event, or whatever it is that is causing you strife. If money is the issue, visualize a 50-dollar bill or euro note. If you're not a visual person, imagine the feeling surrounding the issue. Now, move your mind forward one month. For example, if you are arguing with a friend, jump your mind ahead one month. Is the fight still going on? If so, move your mind another month, or perhaps yet another, until it is over. If money is the problem, visualize that bill in color and moving forward on your timeline until it's something that is flowing towards you.

Now, ask your mind, "How may I resolve this issue please?" Listen to what your mind says even if it's not all that clear at first. Somewhere in there will be a symbol or an answer to your question. If you don't receive the answer, ask your mind to give it to you in your dreams while you sleep. This is a very powerful exercise because it teaches you how to talk to your mind, which allows it to share deep insight with you and ease your stress. If you look at what your mind is creating, you will be looking at your life. You will be able to understand how to change it for the better.

ABOUT THE AUTHOR

For more than 20 years, Derek O'Neill has been transforming the lives of thousands of people around the world for the better. An internationally acclaimed transformational coach and therapist, motivational speaker, author, martial arts sensei and humanitarian, Derek inspires and uplifts people from all walks of life through his workshops, consultations, speaking engagements, media, and tireless humanitarian work.

Drawing on thirty years of training in martial arts, which earned him the level of Master Black Belt, coupled with his extraordinary intuitive abilities and expertise as a psychotherapist, Derek has pioneered a new psychology, transformational therapy. His signature process, aptly named "The Sword and the Brush," helps clients to seamlessly transmute their struggles into positive outcomes, using the sword to cut away old patterns and the brush to help paint the picture of the new life that they require.

In addition to reaching large audiences through workshops and media, Derek advises individuals, celebrities, business leaders, and politicians, helping them to find new perspectives on long-standing issues and bringing harmony back to their lives and businesses.

Author of More Truth Will Set You Free, the Get a Grip series of pocket books, a cutting edge book on parenting titled Calm Mama,

Happy Baby, and several children's books, Derek also hosted his own radio show, "The Way With Derek O'Neill," which enjoyed the most successful launch in VoiceAmerica's history, quickly garnering 100,000 listeners.

Derek is a master at offering practical wisdom and proven techniques for living a more harmonious and fulfilling life, bringing CEOs to the level of wise yogi and wise yogis to CEO; he has worked with executives from some of the world's major airlines, and the cast of Spiderman on Broadway to help transform group disharmony and untapped creative potential into productivity and dynamic performance. He has been featured in Exceptional People Magazine, The Irish Independent, The Irish Examiner, CBS television, and RTE, Ireland's national TV network.

Inspired by his worldly travels, he formed SQ Foundation, a not-for-profit organization focused on helping to solve global issues facing humanity today. In 2012, he was honored as Humanitarian of the Year and named International Celebrity Ambassador for Variety International the Children's Charity. He was welcomed as Vice President of the esteemed charity in May 2013.

Recordings of Derek's discourses are available for download, offering practical wisdom and proven techniques for living a more harmonious and fulfilling life.

To learn more about Derek O'Neill, to attend his next workshop, to order books, downloads or to contact him, please visit his website:

derekoneill.com

To learn more about SQ Foundation, the global charity that is changing the lives of hundreds of thousands of people around the world, go to:

sq-foundation.org

MORE RESOURCES FROM DEREK O'NEILL

Books

Calm Mama, Happy Baby

Get a Grip Book Series

Happiness - You Must Be Effin' Joking!

Anger – Who Gives a Shite?

Relationships – Would You Want to Date You?

Depression – What's that?

Weight – What's Eating You?

Confidence – Easy for You to Say

Abundance – Starts Right Now

Fear - A Powerful Illusion

Addiction - What a Cover-Up!

Excellence - You Never Lost It, You Forgot It

Grief - Mind Boggling, but Natural

Suicide - Fast or Slow

Stress - Is stress stressing you out?

Children's Books

Water Drop Coloring Book

The Adventures of Lucinda in Love-Filled Fairyland

SOCIAL MEDIA

YouTube
youtube.com/user/DerekONeill101

Facebook
facebook.com/derekoneill101

Twitter
twitter.com/DerekONeill101

LinkedIn
linkedin.com/in/derekoneill101